The Quotable Emerson

Life lessons from the words of Ralph Waldo Emerson

Over 300 quotes

By Richard W. Willoughby

Our best thoughts come from others. **Emerson**

Please visit our free blog On Emerson at:

http://emersonsaidit.blogspot.com/

We support the Emerson Society.
For more information please go to:

WWW. EmersOnsociety.org

A short biography of Ralph Waldo Emerson
By his son
Edward W. Emerson

Edward Waldo Emerson (1844-1930)—the youngest child of philosopher, lecturer, essayist, and poet Ralph Waldo Emerson and his second wife Lidian (Jackson) Emerson—lived most of his life in Concord, Massachusetts.

As a child, he grew close to Henry David Thoreau, who presided over the Emerson household as a live-in caretaker while Ralph Waldo Emerson traveled in Europe in 1847 and 1848.

Edward attended Frank Sanborn's progressive, coeducational Concord private school. Rejected for service during the Civil War because of fragile health, Edward went to college instead of war, graduating from Harvard in 1866.

Although artistic, he bowed to practical considerations and studied medicine. He spent a year in Berlin and London while enrolled at Harvard Medical School, from which he graduated in 1874.

Back in Concord, he assisted Dr. Josiah Bartlett, eventually taking over Bartlett's practice. After his father's death in 1882, Edward left the practice of medicine and spent his time writing, editing his father's papers and manuscripts, and painting.

He wrote the Social Circle biography of his father (1888), *Henry Thoreau as Remembered by a Young Friend* (1917), and edited his father's correspondence.

In 1874, Edward married Concord girl Annie Shepard Keyes, daughter of John Shepard and Martha (Prescott) Keyes. They had seven children, six of whom predeceased their parents. Edward Emerson served Concord as Superintendent of Schools and on the Board of Health, the Cemetery Committee, and the Library Committee.

A Brief Biography of Ralph Waldo Emerson

The Emersons first appeared in the north of England, but Thomas, who landed in Massachusetts in 1638, came from Hertfordshire. He built soon after a house, sometimes railed the Saint's Rest, which still stands in Ipswich on the slope of Heart-break Hill, close by Labour-in-vain Creek.

Ralph Waldo Emerson was the sixth in descent from him. He was born in Boston, in Summer Street, May 25, 1803. He was the third son of William Emerson, the minister of the First Church in Boston, whose father, William Emerson, had been the patriotic minister of Concord at the outbreak of the Revolution, and died a chaplain in the army. Ruth Haskins, the mother of Ralph Waldo Emerson, was left a widow in 1811,
with a family of five little boys.

The taste of these boys was scholarly, and four of them went through the Latin School to Harvard College, and graduated there. Their mother was a person of great sweetness, dignity, and piety, bringing up her sons wisely and well in very straitened circumstances, and loved by them. Her husband's stepfather, Rev. Dr. Ripley of Concord, helped her, and constantly invited the boys to the Old Manse, so that the woods and fields along
the Concord River were first a playground and then the background of the dreams of their awakening imaginations.

Born in the city, Emerson's young mind first found delight in poems and classic prose, to which his instincts led him as naturally as another boy's would to go fishing, but his vacations in the country supplemented these by giving him great and increasing love of nature.

In his early poems classic imagery is woven into pictures of New England woodlands.
Even as a little boy he had the habit of attempting flights of verse, stimulated by Milton, Pope, or Scott, and he and his mates took pleasure in declaiming to each

other in barns and attics. He was so full of thoughts and fancies that he sought the pen instinctively, to jot them down.

At college Emerson did not shine as a scholar, though he won prizes for essays and declamations, being especially unfitted for mathematical studies, and enjoying the classics rather in a literary than grammatical way. And yet it is doubtful whether any man in his class used his time to better purpose with reference to his after life, for young Emerson's instinct led him to wide reading of works, outside the curriculum, that
spoke directly to him.
He had already formed the habit of writing in a journal, not the facts but the thoughts and inspirations of the day; often, also, good stories or poetical quotations, and scraps of his own verse.

On graduation from Harvard in the class of 1821, following the traditions of his family, Emerson resolved to study to be a minister and meantime helped his older brother William in the support of the family by teaching in a school for young ladies in Boston that the former had successfully established. The principal was twenty-one and the assistant nineteen years of age.

For school-teaching on the usual lines Emerson was not fitted, and his youth and shyness prevented him from imparting his best gifts to his scholars. Years later, when, in his age, his old scholars assembled to greet him, he regretted that no hint
had been brought into the school of what at that very time "I was writing every night in my chamber, my first thoughts on morals and the beautiful laws of

compensation, and of individual genius, which to observe and illustrate have given sweetness to many years of my life."

Yet many scholars remembered his presence and teaching with pleasure and gratitude, not only in Boston, but in Chelmsford and Roxbury, for while his younger brothers were in college it was necessary that he should help. In these years, as through all his youth, he was loved, spurred on in his intellectual life, and keenly criticized by his aunt, Mary Moody Emerson, an eager and wide reader, inspired by religious zeal,
high-minded, but eccentric.

The health of the young teacher suffered from too ascetic a life, and unmistakable danger-signals began to appear, fortunately heeded in time, but disappointment and delay resulted, borne, however, with sense and courage. His course at the Divinity School in Cambridge was much broken; nevertheless, in October, 1826, he was "approbated to preach" by the Middlesex Association of Ministers.

A winter at the North at this time threatened to prove fatal, so he was sent South by his helpful kinsman, Rev. Samuel Ripley, and passed the winter in Florida with benefit,
working northward in the spring, preaching in the cities, and resumed his studies at Cambridge.

In 1829, Emerson was called by the Second or Old North Church in Boston to become the associate pastor with Rev. Henry Ware, and soon after, because of his senior's delicate health, was called on to assume the full duty. Theological dogmas, such as the Unitarian Church of Channing's day accepted, did not appeal to Emerson, nor did the supernatural in religion in its ordinary acceptation interest him.

 The omnipresence of spirit, the dignity of man, the daily miracle of the universe, were what he taught, and while the older members of the congregation may have been disquieted that he did not dwell on revealed religion, his words reached the young people, stirred thought, and awakened aspiration. At this time he lived with his mother and his young wife (Ellen Tucker) in Chardon Street.

For three years he ministered to his people in Boston. Then having felt the shock of being obliged to conform to church usage, as stated prayer when the spirit did not move, and especially the administration of the Communion, he honestly laid his troubles before his people, and proposed to them some modification of this rite.

While they considered his proposition, Emerson went into the White Mountains to weigh his conflicting duties to his church and conscience. He came down, bravely to meet the refusal of the church to change the rite, and in a sermon preached in September, 1832, explained his objections to it, and, because he could not honestly administer it, resigned.

He parted from his people in all kindness, but the wrench was felt. His wife had recently died, he was ill himself, his life seemed to others broken up. But meantime voices from far away had reached him. He sailed for Europe, landed in Italy, saw cities, and art, and men, but would not stay long.

Of the dead, Michael Angelo appealed chiefly to him there; Landor among the living. He soon passed northward, making little stay in Paris, but sought out Carlyle, then hardly recognized, and living in the lonely hills of the Scottish Border. There began a friendship which had great influence on the lives of both men, and lasted through life. He also visited Wordsworth. But the new life before him called him home.

He landed at Boston within the year in good health and hope, and joined his mother and youngest brother Charles in Newton. Frequent invitations to preach still came, and were accepted, and he even was sounded as to succeeding Dr. Dewey in the church at New Bedford; but, as he stipulated for freedom from ceremonial, this came to nothing.

In the autumn of 1834 he moved to Concord, living with his kinsman, Dr. Ripley, at the Manse, but soon bought house and land on the Boston Road, on the edge of the village towards Walden woods. Thither, in the autumn, he brought his wife. Miss Lidian Jackson, of Plymouth, and this was their home during the rest of their lives.

The new life to which he had been called opened pleasantly and increased in happiness and opportunity, except for the sadness of bereavements, for, in the first few years, his brilliant brothers Edward and Charles died, and soon afterward Waldo, his firstborn son, and later his mother.

Emerson had left traditional religion, the city, the Old World, behind, and now went to Nature as his teacher, his inspiration. His first book, "Nature," which he was meditating while in Europe, was finished here, and published in 1836. His practice during all his life in Concord was to go alone to the woods almost daily, sometimes to wait there for
hours, and, when thus attuned, to receive the message to which he was to give voice. Though it might be colored by him in transmission, he held that the light was universal.

> "Ever the words of the Gods resound,
> But the porches of man's ear
> Seldom in this low life's round
> Are unsealed that he may hear."

But he resorted, also, to the books of those who had handed down the oracles truly, and was quick to find the message destined for him. Men, too, he studied eagerly, the humblest and the highest, regretting always that the brand of the scholar on him often silenced the men of shop and office where he came.

He was everywhere a learner, expecting light from the youngest and least educated visitor. The thoughts combined with the flower of his reading were gradually grouped into lectures, and his main occupation through life was reading these to who would hear, at first in courses in Boston, but later all over the country, for the Lyceum sprang
up in New England in these years in every town, and spread westward to the new settlements even beyond the Mississippi.

His winters were spent in these rough, but to him interesting journeys, for he loved to watch the growth of the Republic in which he had faith, and his summers were spent in study and writing. These lectures were later severely pruned and revised, and the best of them gathered into seven volumes of essays under different names between 1841 and 1876.

The courses in Boston, which at first were given in the Masonic Temple, were always well attended by earnest and thoughtful people. The young, whether in years or in spirit, were always and to the end his audience of the spoken or written word. The freedom of the Lyceum platform pleased Emerson. He found that people would hear on Wednesday with approval and unsuspectingly doctrines from which on Sunday they felt officially obliged to dissent.

Mr. Lowell, in his essays, has spoken of these early lectures and what they were worth to him and others suffering from the generous discontent of youth with things as they were. Emerson used to say, "My strength and my doom is to be solitary;" but to a retired scholar a wholesome offset to this was the travelling and lecturing in cities and in raw frontier towns, bringing him into touch with the people, and this he knew and valued.

In 1837 Emerson gave the Phi Beta Kappa oration in Cambridge, The American Scholar, which increased his growing reputation, but the following year his Address to the Senior Class at the Divinity School brought out, even from the friendly Unitarians, severe strictures and warnings against its dangerous doctrines. Of this heresy Emerson said:
"I deny personality to God because it is too little, not too much."

He really strove to elevate the idea of God. Yet those who were pained or shocked by his teachings respected Emerson. His lectures were still in demand; he was often asked to speak by literary societies at orthodox colleges. He preached regularly at East Lexington until 1838, but thereafter withdrew from the ministerial office.

At this time the progressive and spiritually minded young people used to meet for discussion and help in Boston, among them George Ripley, Cyrus Bartol, James Freeman Clarke, Alcott, Dr. Hedge, Margaret Fuller, and Elizabeth Peabody. Perhaps from this gathering of friends, which Emerson attended, came what is called the Transcendental Movement, two results of which were the Brook Farm Community and the Dial magazine, in which last Emerson took great interest, and was for the time an editor.

Many of these friends were frequent visitors in Concord. Alcott moved thither after the breaking up of his school. Hawthorne also came to dwell there. Henry Thoreau, a Concord youth, greatly interested Emerson; indeed, became for a year or two a valued inmate of his home, and helped and instructed him in the labors of the garden and little farm, which gradually grew to ten acres, the chief interest of which for the owner
was his trees, which he loved and tended. Emerson helped introduce his countrymen to the teachings of Carlyle, and edited his works here, where they found more readers than at home.

In 1847 Emerson was invited to read lectures in England, and remained abroad a year, visiting France also in her troublous times. English Traits was a result. Just before this journey he had collected and published his poems. A later volume, called May Day, followed in 1867.

He had written verses from childhood, and to the purified expression of poetry he, through life, eagerly aspired. He said, "I like my poems best because it is not I who write them." In 1866 the degree of Doctor of Laws was conferred on him by Harvard University, and he was chosen an Overseer. In 1867 he again gave the Phi Beta Kappa oration, and in 1870 and 1871 gave courses in Philosophy in the University Lectures at
Cambridge.

Emerson was not merely a man of letters. He recognized and did the private and public duties of the hour. He exercised a wide hospitality to souls as well as bodies. Eager youths came to him for rules, and went away with light. Reformers, wise and unwise, came to him, and were kindly received. They were often disappointed that they could not harness him to their partial and transient scheme.

He said, My reforms include theirs: I must go my way; help people by my strength, not by my weakness. But if a storm threatened, he felt bound to appear and show his colors. Against the crying evils of his time he worked bravely in his own way. He wrote to President Van Buren against the wrong done to the Cherokees, dared speak against the idolized Webster, when he deserted the cause of Freedom, constantly spoke of the iniquity of slavery, aided with speech and money the Free State cause in Kansas,
was at Phillips's side at the antislavery meeting in 1861 broken up by the Boston mob, urged emancipation during the war.

He enjoyed his Concord home and neighbors, served on the school committee for years, did much for the Lyceum, and spoke on the town's great occasions. He went to all town-meetings, oftener to listen and admire than to speak, and always took pleasure and pride in the people. In return he was respected and loved by them.

Emerson's house was destroyed by fire in 1872, and the incident exposure and fatigue did him harm. His many friends insisted on rebuilding his house and sending him abroad to get well. He went up the Nile, and revisited England, finding old and new friends, and, on his return, was welcomed and escorted home by the people of Concord. After this time he was unable to write. His old age was quiet and happy among his family and friends. He died in April, 1882.

EDWARD W. EMERSON.

January, 1899.

A

On achievement

Every great achievement is the victory of a flaming heart.

On Americans

I find that the Americans have no passions they have appetites.

On Actions

There is a tendency for things to right themselves.

On anger

One ought never to turn One's back On a threatened danger and try to run away from it. If you do that you will double the danger. But if you meet it promptly and without flinching you will reduce the danger by half. Never run away from anything. Never!

As soon as there is life there is danger.

The wise man in the storm prays to God not for safety from danger but for deliverance from fear.

On adventure

The thirst for adventure is the vent which Destiny offers; a war a crusade a gold mine a new country speak to the imagination and offer swing and play to the confined powers.

On action (Taking action)

Do not be too timid and squeamish about your actions. All life is an experiment.

Act if you like but you do it at your peril. Men's actions are too strong for them. Show me a man who has acted and who has not been the victim and slave of his action.

The German intellect wants the French sprightliness the fine practical understanding of the English and the American adventure; but it has a certain probity which never rests in a superficial performance but asks steadily To what end? A German public asks for a controlling sincerity.

Let us if we must have great actions make our own so. All action is of infinite elasticity and the least admits of being inflated with celestial air until it eclipses the sun and moon.

Men's actions are too strong for them. Show me a man who has acted and who has not been the victim and slave of his action.

The ancestor of every action is thought.

Real action is in silent moments.

We are taught by great actions that the universe is the property of every individual in it.

Thought is the blossom; language the bud; action the fruit behind it.

We are always getting ready to live but never living.

Why should we be cowed by the name of Action?

A man's action is only a picture book of his creed.

On autobiographies (Life reflections see also "On biography")

It is long ere we discover how rich we are. Our history we are sure is quite tame: we have nothing to write nothing to infer. But our wiser years still run back to the despised recollections of childhood and always we are fishing up some wonderful article out of that pond; until by and by we begin to suspect that the biography of the One foolish person we know is in reality nothing less than the miniature paraphrase of the hundred volumes of the Universal History.

On adversity (Facing adversity)

Out of love and hatred out of earnings and borrowings and leadings and losses; out of sickness and pain; out of wooing and worshipping; out of traveling and voting and watching and caring; out of disgrace and contempt comes our tuition in the serene and beautiful laws.

Most of the shadows of this life are caused by standing in One's own sunshine

A man is a god in ruins.

On affection

The moment we indulge our affections the earth is metamorphosed there is no winter and no night; all tragedies all ennui s vanish all duties even.

On age and aging

We do not count a man's years until he has nothing else to count.

Nature is full of freaks and now puts an old head on young shoulders and then takes a young heart heating under fourscore winters.

On ability

People with great gifts are easy to find but symmetrical and balanced Ones never.

Big jobs usually go to the men who prove their ability to outgrow small Ones.

On achievement

To be yourself in a world that is constantly trying to make you something else is the greatest accomplishment.

Finish each day and be done with it. You have done what you could. Some blunders and absurdities no doubt crept in; forget them as soon as you can. Tomorrow is a new day; begin it well and serenely and with too high a spirit to be encumbered with your old nonsense.

On assistance

We do not quite forgive a giver. The hand that feeds us is in some danger of being bitten.

On alcohol

There is this to be said in favor of drinking that it takes the drunkard first out of society then out of the world.

On ambition

Without ambition One starts nothing. Without work one finishes nothing. The prize will not be sent to you. You have to win it. The man who knows how will always have a job. The man who also knows why will always be his boss. As to methods there may be a million and then some but principles are few. The man who grasps principles can successfully select his own methods. The man who tries methods ignoring principles is sure to have trouble.

On amusement

The intellectual man requires a fine bait; the sots are easily amused. But everybody is drugged with his own frenzy and the pageant marches at all hours with music and banner and badge.

On ancestry

Good breeding a union of kindness and independence.

On angels

The angels are so enamored of the language that is spoken in heaven that they will not distort their lips with the hissing and unmusical dialects of men but speak their own whether there be any who understand it or not.

On art

His heart was as great as the world but there was no room in it to hold the memory of a wrong.

Great hearts steadily send forth the secret forces that incessantly draw great events.

The arts and inventions of each period are only its costume and do not invigorate men.

The true poem is the poet's mind.

Sculpture and painting have the effect of teaching us manners and abolishing hurry.

Perpetual modernness is the measure of merit in every work of art.

New arts destroy the old.

Classic art was the art of necessity: modern romantic art bears the stamp of caprice and chance.

Art is a jealous mistress; and if a man have a genius for painting poetry music architecture or philosophy he makes a bad husband and an ill provider.

Art is the path of the creator to his work.

Each work of art excludes the world concentrates attention On itself. For the time it is the Only thing worth doing --to do just that; be it a sonnet a statue a landscape an outline head of Caesar or an oration. Presently we return to the sight of another that globes itself into a whole as did the first for example a beautiful garden; and nothing seems worth doing in life but laying out a garden.

The True Artist has the planet for his pedestal; the adventurer after years of strife has nothing broader than his shoes.

Every artist was first an amateur.

Artists must be sacrificed to their art.

On anger

A man makes inferiors his superiors by heat; self-control is the rule.

We boil at different degrees.

For every minute you are angry you lose sixty seconds of happiness.

On animals

Who can guess how much industry and providence and affection we have caught from the pantomime of brutes?

On anxiety

Some of your grief you have cured and lived to survive; but what torments of pain have you endured that haven't as yet arrived.

On appearance

'Tis very certain that each man carries in his eye the exact indication of his rank in the immense scale of men and we are always learning to read it. A complete man should need no auxiliaries to his personal presence.

On attitude

To different minds the same world is a hell and a heaven.

B

On babies

Infancy conforms to nobody: all conform to it so that One babe commonly makes four or five out of the adults who prattle and play to it.

On beauty

We ascribe beauty to that which is simple; which has no superfluous parts; which exactly answers its end; which stands related to all things; which is the mean of many extremes.

The line of beauty is the line of perfect economy.

Beauty rests on necessities.

As soon as beauty is sought not from religion and love but for pleasure it degrades the seeker.

Beauty is the mark God sets On virtue. Every natural action is graceful; every heroic act is also decent and causes the place and the bystanders to shine.

Beauty is the pilot of the young soul.

A beautiful form is better than a beautiful face; it gives a higher pleasure than statues or pictures; it is the finest of the fine arts.

On beginnings

The great majority of men are bundles of beginnings.

On belief

Belief consists in accepting the affirmations of the soul; unbelief in denying them.

We are born believing. A man bears beliefs as a tree bears apples.

All the great ages have been ages of belief.

On bereavement

The death of a dear friend wife brother lover which seemed nothing but privation somewhat later assumes the aspect of a guide or genius; for it commonly operates revolutions in our way of life terminates an epoch of infancy or of youth which was waiting to be closed breaks up a wonted occupation or a household or style of living and allows the formation of new Ones more friendly to the growth of character.

On bigotry and indifference

Religion is as effectually destroyed by bigotry as by indifference.

On biography

Great geniuses have the shortest biographies.

There is properly no history; only biography.

On Books (classics)

There are books which take rank in your life with parents and lovers and passionate experiences so medicinal so stringent so revolutionary so authoritative.

On books – (reading)

If we encounter a man of rare intellect we should ask him what books he reads.

Never read any book that is not a year old.

Our high respect for a well-read person is praise enough for literature.

Books are the best of things if well used; if abused among the worst. They are good for nothing but to inspire. I had better never see a book than be warped by its attraction clean out of my own orbit and made a satellite instead of a system.

'Tis the good reader that makes the good book; in every book he finds passages which seem to be confidences or sides hidden from all else and unmistakably meant for his ear; the profit of books is according to the sensibility of the reader; the profound thought or passion sleeps as in a mine until it is discovered by an equal mind and heart.

We are too civil to books. For a few golden sentences we will turn over and actually read a volume of four or five hundred pages.

Some books leave us free and some books make us free.

There is creative reading as well as creative writing.

On bragging

If I cannot brag of knowing something then I brag of not knowing it; at any rate brag.

There is also this benefit in brag that the speaker is unconsciously expressing his own ideal. Humor him by all means draw it all out and hold him to it.

On business

Every man is a consumer and ought to be a producer.

The right merchant is One who has the just average of faculties we call common sense; a man of a strong affinity for facts who makes up his decision On what he has seen. He is thoroughly persuaded of the truths of arithmetic. There is always a reason in the man for his good or bad fortune in making money. Men talk as if there were some magic about this. He knows that all goes On the old road pound for pound cent for cent -- for every effect a perfect cause -- and that good luck is another name for tenacity of purpose.

C

On children

There never was a child so lovely but his mother was glad to get him asleep.

The child with his sweet pranks the fool of his senses commanded by every sight and sound without any power to compare and rank his sensations abandoned to a whistle or a painted chip to a lead dragon or a gingerbread dog individualizing everything generalizing nothing delighted with every new thing lies down at night overpowered by the fatigue which this day of continual pretty madness has incurred. But Nature has answered her purpose with the curly dimpled lunatic.

She has tasked every faculty and has secured the symmetrical growth of the bodily frame by all these attitudes and exertions --an end of the first importance which could not be trusted to any care less perfect than her own.

On choice

Trust your instinct to the end though you can render no reason.

We are as much informed of a writer's genius by what he selects as by what he originates.

On criticism

Manifold allusion. Every sentence is doubly significant and the sense of our author is as broad as the world.

On calamity

Every calamity is a spur and valuable hint.

On censorship

Every burned book or house enlightens the world; every suppressed or expunged word reverberates through the earth from side to side.

On change

People wish to be settled. It is only as far as they are unsettled that there is any hope for them.

On character

No change of circumstances can repair a defect of character.

Judge of your natural character by what you do in dreams.

Character is higher than intellect. A great soul will be strong to live as well as think.

People seem not to see that their opinion of the world is also a confession of character.

That which we call character is a reserved force which acts directly by presence and without means. It is conceived of as a certain undemonstrable force a familiar or genius by whose impulses the man is guided but whose counsels he cannot impart.

Make the most of yourself for that is all there is of you.

Gross and obscure natures however decorated seem impure shambles; but character gives splendor to youth and awe to wrinkled skin and gray hairs.

Do what you know and perception is converted into character.

A character is like an acrostic or Alexandrian stanza; read it forward backward or across it still spells the same thing.

On charity

Give no bounties: make equal laws: secure life and prosperity and you need not give alms.

Do not tell me of my obligation to put all poor men in good situations. Are they my poor? I tell thee thou foolish philanthropist that I grudge the dollar the dime the cent I give to such men as do not belong to me and to whom I do not belong.

On cheerfulness

So of cheerfulness or a good temper the more it is spent the more it remains.

On civilization

As long as our civilization is essentially One of property of fences of exclusiveness it will be mocked by delusions. Our riches will leave us sick; there will be bitterness in our laughter; and our wine will burn our mouth. Only that good profits which we can taste with all doors open and which serves all men.

Sunday is the core of our civilization dedicated to thought and reverence.

Civilization depends on morality.

On college

One of the benefits of a college education is to show the boy its little avail.

Universities are of course hostile to geniuses which seeing and using ways of their own discredit the routine: as churches and monasteries persecute youthful saints.

The colleges while they provide us with libraries furnish no professors of books; and I think no chair is so much needed.

On comedy

The perception of the comic is a tie of sympathy with other men a pledge of sanity and a protection from those perverse tendencies and gloomy insanities in which fine intellects sometimes lose themselves. A rogue alive to the ludicrous is still convertible. If that sense is lost his fellow-men can do little for him.

On commitment

All great masters are chiefly distinguished by the power of adding a second a third and perhaps a fourth step in a continuous line. Many a man had taken the first step. With every additional step you enhance immensely the value of your first.

On common sense

Common sense is genius dressed in its working clothes.

Nothing astonishes people so much as common sense and plain dealing.

On communication

When the eyes say one thing and the tongue another a practiced man relies On the language of the first.

On compensation

For everything you have missed you have gained something else; and for everything you gain you lose something else.

On complaints

There is One topic peremptorily forbidden to all well-bred to all rational mortals namely their distempers. If you have not slept or if you have slept or if you have headache or sciatica or leprosy or thunder-stroke I beseech you by all angels to hold your peace and not pollute the morning.

On conceit

Solvency is maintained by means of a national debt on the principle If you will not lend me the money how can I pay you?

On conflict

We know better than we do. We do not yet possess ourselves...

We are the prisoners of ideas.

On conformity

One lesson we learn early that in spite of seeming difference men are all of One pattern. We readily assume this with our mates and are disappointed and angry if we find that we are premature and that their watches are slower than ours. In fact the only sin which we never forgive in each other is difference of opinion.

On consequences

All successful men have agreed in One thing -- they were causationists. They believed that things went not by luck but by law; that there was not a weak or a cracked link in the chain that joins the first and last of things.

On conservatives

All conservatives are such from personal defects. They have been effeminated by position or nature born halt and blind through luxury of their parents and can Only like invalids act On the defensive.

Men are conservatives when they are least vigorous or when they are most luxurious. They are conservatives after dinner or before taking their rest; when they are sick or aged. In the morning or when their intellect or their conscience has been aroused when they hear music or when they read poetry they are radicals.

On consistency

A foolish consistency is the hobgoblin of little minds adored by little statesmen and philosophers and divines.

On consultants

In every society some men are born to rule and some to advise.

On contradiction

Wise men are not wise at all hours and will speak five times from their taste or their humor to Once from their reason.

Let me never fall into the vulgar mistake of dreaming that I am persecuted whenever I am contradicted.

On control

As the Sandwich Islander believes that the strength and valor of the enemy he kills passes into himself so we gain the strength of the temptation we resist.

Nothing external to you has any power over you.

On conventionality

He who would be a man must therefore be a non-conformist.

On conversation

Things said for conversation are chalk eggs. Don't say things. What you are stands over you the while and thunders so that I cannot hear what you say to the contrary.

In conversation the game is to say something new with old words. And you shall observe a man of the people picking his way along step by step using every time an old boulder yet never setting his foot on an old place.

Conversation is an art in which a man has all mankind for competitors.

On country

Shall we then judge a country by the majority or by the minority? By the minority surely. 'Tis pedantry to estimate nations by the census or by square miles of land or other than by their importance to the mind of the time.

On courage

Courage charms us because it indicates that a man loves an idea better than all things in the world that he is thinking neither of his bed nor his dinner nor his money but will venture all to put in act the invisible thought of his mind.

Courage consists in equality to the problem before us.

A great part of courage is the courage of having done the thing before.

When a resolute young fellow steps up to the great bully the world and takes him boldly by the beard he is often surprised to find it comes off in his hand and that it was Only tied On to scare away the timid adventurers.

Whatever you do you need courage. Whatever course you decide upon there is always someone to tell you that you are wrong. There are always difficulties arising that tempt you to believe your critics are right. To map out a course of action and follow it to an end requires some of the same courage that a soldier needs. Peace has its victories but it takes brave men and women to win them.

What a new face courage puts On everything!

Half a man's wisdom goes with his courage.

On courtesy

We must be as courteous to a man as we are to a picture which we are willing to give the advantage of a good light.

Life is short but there is always time for courtesy.

Courtesy Life be not so short but that there is always time for courtesy.

On crafts

It is the privilege of any human work which is well done to invest the doer with a certain haughtiness. He can well afford not to conciliate whose faithful work will answer for him.

On creativity

That which builds is better than that which is built.

On creeds

As men's prayers are a disease of the will so are their creeds a disease of the intellect.

On crime and criminals

Crime and punishment grow out of one stem. Punishment is a fruit that unsuspected ripens with the flower of the pleasure that concealed it.

Commit a crime and the earth is made of glass.

On criticism

Blame is safer than praise.

Criticism should not be querulous and wasting all knife and root-puller but guiding instructive inspiring.

On culture

Culture is one thing and varnish is another.

On curiosity

Curiosity is lying in wait for every secret.

On curses

Curses always recoil on the head of him who imprecates them. If you put a chain around the neck of a slave the other end fastens itself around your own.

On cynics and cynicism

Don't be a cynic and disconsolate preacher. Don't bewail and moan. Omit the negative propositions. Challenge us with incessant affirmatives. Don't waste yourself in rejection or bark against the bad but chant the beauty of the good.

A cynic can chill and dishearten with a single word.

D

On debt

It is said that the world is in a state of bankruptcy that the world owes the world more than the world can pay.

On decisions

Once you make a decision the universe conspires to make it happen.

On dependence

The ship of heaven guides itself and will not accept a wooden rudder.

On desire

There is nothing capricious in nature and the implanting of a desire indicates that its gratification is in the constitution of the creature that feel it.

Can anything be so elegant as to have few wants and to serve them One's self?

On destiny

Sow a thought and you reap an action; sow an act and you reap a habit; sow a habit and you reap a character; sow a character and you reap a destiny.

Fate then is a name for facts not yet passed under the fire of thought; for causes which are unpenetrated.

On diets

'Tis a superstition to insist on a special diet. All is made at last of the same chemical atoms.

On difficulties

When it is dark enough you can see the stars.

There are always difficulties arising that tempt you to believe your critics are right.

Can anybody remember when the times were not hard and money not scarce?

Bad times have a scientific value. These are occasions a good learner would not miss.

On disasters

The compensations of calamity are made apparent to the understanding also after long intervals of time. A fever a mutilation a cruel disappointment a loss of wealth a loss of friends seems at the moment unpaid loss and unpayable. But the sure years reveal the deep remedial force that underlies all facts.

On discipline

Self-command is the main discipline.

On discovery

If a man knew anything he would sit in a corner and be modest; but he is such an ignorant peacock that he goes bustling up and down and hits On extraordinary discoveries.

On disease

All diseases run into one. Old age.

On action

There are three wants which never can be satisfied: that of the rich who wants something more; that of the sick who wants something different; and that of the traveler who says anywhere but here.

On dress

I have heard with admiring submission the experience of the lady who declared that the sense of being perfectly well dressed gives a feeling of inward tranquility which religion is powerless to bestow.

On drugs

Tobacco and opium have broad backs and will cheerfully carry the load of armies if you choose to make them pay high for such joy as they give and such harm as they do.

On duty

Do that which is assigned to you and you cannot hope too much or dare too much.

E

On evolution

Every revolution was first a thought in one man's mind.

If there is any period one would desire to be born in is it not the age of Revolution; when the old and the new stand side by side and admit of being compared; when the energies of all men are searched by fear and by hope; when the historic glories of the old can be compensated by the rich possibilities of the new era?

On economy and economics

Commerce is a game of skill which everyone cannot play and few can play well.

On education

I pay the schoolmaster but it is the school boys who educate my son.

Respect the child. Be not too much his parent. Trespass not on his solitude.

The secret in education lies in respecting the student.

There is a time in every man's education when he arrives at the conviction that envy is ignorance; that imitation is suicide.

We are shut up in schools and college recitation rooms for ten or fifteen years and come out at last with a belly-full of words and do not know a thing. The things taught in schools and colleges are not an education but the means of education.

On egotism

The pest of society are the egotist they are dull and bright sacred and profane course and fine. It is a disease that like the flu falls on all constitutions.

On eloquence

The eloquent man is he who is no eloquent speaker but who is inwardly drunk with a certain belief.

On empire

An empire is an immense egotism.

On energy

Coal is a portable climate. It carries the heat of the tropics to Labrador and the polar circle; and it is the means of transporting itself whithersoever it is wanted. Watt and Stephenson whispered in the ear of mankind their secret that a half-ounce of coal will draw two tons a mile and coal carries coal by rail and by boat to make Canada as warm as Calcutta and with its comfort brings its industrial power.

On enthusiasm

Nothing great was ever achieved without enthusiasm.

Every great and commanding movement in the annals of the world is due to the triumph of enthusiasm. Nothing great was ever achieved without it.

Enthusiasm is the leaping lightning not to be measured by the horse-power of the understanding.

Enthusiasm is the mother of effort and without it nothing great was ever achieved.

On envy

Envy is the tax which all distinction must pay.

On equality

Some will always be above others. Destroy the inequality today and it will appear again tomorrow.

On exaggeration

There is no One who does not exaggerate!

'Tis a rule of manners to avoid exaggeration.

On example

The world is upheld by the veracity of good men: they make the earth wholesome. They who lived with them found life glad and nutritious. Life is sweet and tolerable Only in our belief in such society.

On excellence

There is always a best way of doing everything.

On exercise

Few people know how to take a walk. The qualifications are endurance plain clothes old shoes an eye for nature good humor vast curiosity good speech good silence and nothing too much.

Intellectual tasting of life will not supersede muscular activity.

On expectation

How much of human life is lost in waiting.

On experience

Our knowledge is the amassed thought and experience of innumerable minds.

The more experiments you make the better.

On extra mile

I hate the giving of the hand unless the whole man accompanies it.

On eyes

The eye is easily frightened.

The eyes indicate the antiquity of the soul.

F

On faces

A man finds room in the few square inches of the face for the traits of all his ancestors; for the expression of all his history and his wants.

On facts

If a man will kick a fact out of the window when he comes back he finds it again in the chimney corner.

Every fact is related on one side to sensation and on the other two morals. The game of thought is on the appearance of One of these two sides to find the other; given the upper to find the underside.

Time dissipates to shining ether the solid angularity of facts.

No facts are to me sacred; none are profane; I simply experiment an endless seeker with no past at my back.

On faith

Our faith comes in moments... yet there is a depth in those brief moments which constrains us to ascribe more reality to them than to all other experiences.

All that I have seen teaches me to trust the Creator for all I have not seen.

The course of everything goes to teach us faith.

The faith that stands on authority is not faith.

On fame

Fame is proof that the people are gullible.

On familiarity

The hues of the opal the light of the diamond are not to be seen if the eye is too near.

On farming and farmers

The first farmer was the first man. All historic nobility rests on the possession and use of land.

On fate

Whatever limits us we call fate.

If you believe in fate believe in it at least for your good.

Fate is nothing but the deeds committed in a prior state of existence.

On faults

A man's personal defects will commonly have with the rest of the world precisely that importance which they have to himself. If he makes light of them so will other men.

On fear

Fear defeats more people than any other One thing in the world.

Fear always springs from ignorance.

Do the thing we fear and the death of fear is certain.

Always do what you are afraid to do.

On finance

We estimate the wisdom of nations by seeing what they did with their surplus capital.

On flowers

Earth laughs in flowers.

Flowers are a proud assertion that a ray of beauty out-values all the utilities of the world.

On focus

Concentration is the secret of strength in politics in war in trade in short in all the management of human affairs.

The only prudence in life is concentration.

On food and eating

I can reason down or deny everything except this perpetual Belly: feed he must and will and I cannot make him respectable.

Let the stoics say what they please we do not eat for the good of living but because the meat is savory and the appetite is keen.

On fortune

Nature magically suits a man to his fortunes by making them the fruit of his character.

On freedom

Liberty is slow fruit. It is never cheap; it is made difficult because freedom is the accomplishment and perfectness of man.

For what avail the plough or sail Or land or life if freedom fail?

So far as a person thinks; they are free.

Nothing is more disgusting than the crowing about liberty by slaves as most men are and the flippant mistaking for freedom of some paper preamble like a Declaration of Independence or the statute right to vote by those who have never dared to think or to act.

On friends and friendship

Go oft to the house of thy friend for weeds choke the unused path.

The ornament of a house is the friends who frequent it.

We talk of choosing our friends but friends are self-elected

He who has a thousand friends has not a friend to spare And he who has One enemy will meet him everywhere.

Friends such as we desire are dreams and fables.

A true friend is somebody who can make us do what we can.

A friend is a person with whom I may be sincere. Before him I may think aloud.

It is one of the blessings of old friends that you can afford to be stupid with them.

The glory of friendship is not in the outstretched hand nor the kindly smile nor the joy of companionship; it is in the spiritual inspiration that comes to One when he discovers that someone else believes in him and is willing to trust him.

A friend may well be reckoned the masterpiece of nature.

A day for toil an hour for sport but for a friend is life too short.

The Only way to have a friend is to be one.

I do then with my friends as I do with my books. I would have them where I can find them but I seldom use them.

I didn't find my friends; the good Lord gave them to me.

Every man passes his life in the search after friendship.

On funerals

The chief mourner does not always attend the funeral.

G

On generosity

It is always so pleasant to be generous though very vexatious to pay debts.

On genius

Only an inventor knows how to borrow and every man is or should be an inventor.

The greatest genius is the most indebted person.

The hearing ear is always found close to the speaking tongue; and no genius can often utter anything which is not invited and gladly entertained by men around him.

To believe your own thought to believe that what is true for you in your private heart is true for all men -- that is genius.

When Nature has work to be done she creates a genius to do it.

In every work of genius we recognize our own rejected thoughts; they come back to us with a certain alienated majesty.

Coffee is good for talent but genius wants prayer.

Accept your genius and say what you think.

A man of genius is privileged only as far as he is genius. His dullness is as insupportable as any other dullness.

On gentlemen

Repose and cheerfulness are the badge of the gentleman -- repose in energy.

On gifts

The only gift is a portion of thyself.

On goals

We aim above the mark to hit the mark.

Those who cannot tell what they desire or expect still sigh and struggle with indefinite thoughts and vast wishes.

On God

'Tis the old secret of the gods that they come in low disguises.

The dice of God are always loaded.

There is a crack in everything God has made.

On evil

Them meaning of good and bad of better and worse is simply helping or hurting.

On goodness

It is very hard to be simple enough to be good.

On government

The less government we have the better.

On gratitude

I awoke this morning with devout thanksgiving for my friends the old and new.

On greatness

No great man ever complains of want of opportunity.

Not he is great who can alter matter but he who can alter my state of mind.

The essence of greatness is the perception that virtue is enough.

The measure of a master is his success in bringing all men around to his opinion twenty years later.

The search after the great men is the dream of youth and the most serious occupation of manhood.

To be great is to be misunderstood.

A great man stands On God. A small man on a great man.

Great people are they who see that spiritual is stronger than any material force that thoughts rule the world.

He is great who is what he is from nature and who never reminds us of others.

On guests

My evening visitors if they cannot see the clock should find the time in my face.

H

On heaven

Many might go to Heaven with half the labor they go to hell.

On happiness

To fill the hour -- that is happiness.

I look on that man as happy who when there is question of success looks into his work for a reply.

Happiness is a perfume which you cannot pour on someone without getting some On yourself.

On health

Health is the condition of wisdom and the sign is cheerfulness -- an open and noble temper.

Give me health and a day and I will make the pomp of emperors ridiculous.

On heroes and heroism

Every hero becomes a bore at last.

The characteristic of genuine heroism is its persistency. All men have wandering impulses fits and starts of generosity. But when you have resolved to be great abide by yourself and do not weakly try to reconcile yourself with the world. The heroic cannot be the common nor the common the heroic.

On heroes and heroism

A hero is no braver than an ordinary man but he is braver five minutes longer.

Heroism feels and never reasons and therefore is always right.

On history and historians

Our best history is still poetry.

On honesty

It is impossible for a man to be cheated by anyone but himself.

Be true to your own act and congratulate yourself if you have done something strange and extravagant to break the monotony of a decorous age.

On honor

The louder he talked of his honor the faster we counted our spoons.

On humankind

The end of the human race will be that it will eventually die of civilization.

On humor

There is this benefit in brag that the speaker is unconsciously expressing his own ideal. Humor him by all means; draw it all out and hold him to it.

On hypocrisy

At the entrance of a second person hypocrisy begins.

I

On Illusion

The most dangerous thing is illusion.

On ideas

We are prisoners of ideas.

It is a lesson which all history teaches wise men to put trust in ideas and not in circumstances.

Ideas must work through the brains and the arms of good and brave men or they are no better than dreams.

On idleness

There is no prosperity trade art city or great material wealth of any kind but if you trace it home you will find it rooted in a thought of some individual man. --

That man is idle who can do something better.

On imagination

What is the imagination? Only an arm or weapon of the interior energy; Only the precursor of the reason.

The quality of the imagination is to flow and not to freeze.

We live by our imagination our admiration s and our sentiments.

Science does not know its debt to imagination.

There are no days in life so memorable as those which vibrate to some stroke of the imagination.

Imagination is not a talent of some people but is the health of everyone.

On imitation

Imitation is suicide.

On immortality

Higher than the question of our duration is the question of our deserving. Immortality will come too such as are fit for it and he would be a great soul in future must be a great soul now.

On impossibility

Every man is an impossibility until he is born.

On individuality

Our expenses are all for conformity.

A man must consider what a rich realm he abdicates when he becomes a conformist.

On influence

Who shall set a limit to the influence of a human being?

The best efforts of a fine person is felt after we have left their presence.

Every thought which genius and piety throw into the world alters the world.

On inheritance

Of course money will do after its kind and will steadily work to unspiritualize and unchurch the people to whom it was bequeathed.

On inspiration

The torpid artist seeks inspiration at any cost by virtue or by vice by friend or by fiend by prayer or by wine.

On instinct

A few strong instincts and a few plain rules suffice us.

On institutions

An institution is the lengthened shadow of One man.

On integrity

Nothing is at last sacred but the integrity of your own mind.

In failing circumstances no one can be relied on to keep their integrity.

On intelligence and intellectuals

Intellect annuls fate. So far as a man thinks he is free.

A sage is the instructor of a hundred ages.

If a man's eye is On the Eternal his intellect will grow.

One definition of man is an intelligence served by organs.

We lie in the lap of immense intelligence.

On intervention

Everything intercepts us from ourselves.

On intuition

If the single man plant himself indomitably on his instincts and there abide the huge world will come round to him.

On invention and inventor

Man is a shrewd inventor and is ever taking the hint of a new machine from his own structure adapting some secret of his own anatomy in iron wood and leather to some required function in the work of the world.

K

On kindness

You cannot do a kindness too soon for you never know how soon it will be too late.

On kings

If you shoot at a king you must kill him.

On knowledge

I would have the studies elective. Scholarship is to be created not by compulsion but by awakening a pure interest in knowledge. The wise instructor accomplishes this by opening to his pupils precisely the attractions the study has for himself. The marking is a system for schools not for the college; for boys not for men; and it is an ungracious work to put on a professor.

Knowledge is knowing that we cannot know.

Knowledge is the only elegance.

Knowledge comes by eyes always open and working hands; and there is no knowledge that is not power.

L

On language

I like to be beholden to the great metropolitan English speech the sea which receives tributaries from every region under heaven.

On life

Cities force growth and make people talkative and entertaining but they also make them artificial.

Cities give us collision. 'Tis said London and New York take the nonsense out of a man.

The city is recruited from the country.

On love

A low self-love in the parent desires that his child should repeat his character and fortune.

On language

Language is the archives of history.

Language is a city to the building of which every human being brought a stone.

On law and lawyers

Good men must not obey the laws too well.

On law and lawyers

The laws of each are convertible into the laws of any other.

The wise know that foolish legislation is a rope of sand which perishes in the twisting.

The good lawyer is not the man who has an eye to every side and angle of contingency and qualifies all his qualifications but who throws himself On your part so heartily that he can get you out of a scrape.

No law can be sacred to me but that of my nature. Good and bad are but names very readily transferable to that or this; the only right is what is after my own constitution; the only wrong what is against it.

On leadership

Our chief want in life is somebody who will make us do what we can.

The measure of a great leader is their success in bringing everyone around to their opinion twenty years later.

The first thing a great person does is make us realize the insignificance of circumstance.

We are reformers in the spring and summer but in autumn we stand by the old. Reformers in the morning and conservers at night.

On learning

In every man there is something wherein I may learn of him and in that I am his pupil.

We learn geology the morning after the earthquake.

The years teach us much the days never knew.

The studious class are their own victims: they are thin and pale their feet are cold their heads are hot the night is without sleep the day a fear of interruption -- pallor squalor hunger and egotism.

No man ever prayed heartily without learning something.

On libraries

A man's library is a sort of harem.

Be a little careful about your library. Do you foresee what you will do with it? Very little to be sure. But the real question is What it will do with you? You will come here and get books that will open your eyes and your ears and your curiosity and turn you inside out or outside in.

Meek young men grow up in libraries believing it their duty to accept the views which Cicero which Locke which Bacon have given forgetful that Cicero Locke and Bacon were Only young men in libraries when they wrote these books. Hence instead of Man Thinking we have the book-worm.

On lies and lying

Every violation of truth is not Only a sort of suicide in the liar but is a stab at the health of human society.

On life

The life of man is the true romance which when it is valiantly conduced will yield the imagination a higher joy than any fiction.

Life is a perpetual instruction in cause and effect.

If we live truly we shall see truly.

Life is a succession of lessons which must be lived to be understood.

Life too near paralyses art.

Like bees they must put their lives into the sting they give.

Live let live and help live

Nothing is beneath you if it is in the direction of your life.

It is not length of life but depth of life.

On light

Light is the first of painters. There is no object so foul that intense light will not make it beautiful.

On literature

There is then creative reading as well as creative writing. When the mind is braced by labor and invention the page of whatever book we read becomes luminous with

People do not deserve to have good writings; they are so pleased with the bad.

On loneliness

Columbus discovered no isle or key so lonely as himself.

On love

All mankind loves a lover.

The power of love as the basis of a State has never been tried.

Love and you shall be loved. All love is mathematically just as much as the two sides of an algebraic equation.

He who is in love is wise and is becoming wiser sees newly every time he looks at the object beloved drawing from it with his eyes and his mind those virtues which it possesses.

On luck

There is no chance and no anarchy in the universe. All is system and gradation. Every god is there sitting in his sphere.

Shallow people believe in luck and in circumstances; Strong people believe in cause and effect.

M

On machinery

By his machines man can dive and remain under water like a shark; can fly like a hawk in the air; can see atoms like a gnat; can see the system of the universe of Uriel the angel of the sun; can carry whatever loads a ton of coal can lift; can knock down cities with his fist of gunpowder; can recover the history of his race by the medals which the deluge and every creature civil or savage or brute has involuntarily dropped of its existence; and divine the future possibility of the planet and its inhabitants by his perception of laws of nature.

On manners

Good manners are made up of petty sacrifices.

Manners are the happy way of doing things; each Once a stroke of genius or of love --now repeated and hardened into usage. They form at last a rich varnish with which the routine of life is washed and its details adorned. If they are superficial so are the dewdrops which give such depth to the morning meadows.

Manners require time and nothing is more vulgar than haste.

The basis of good manners is self-reliance.

There are men whose manners have the same essential splendor as the simple and awful sculpture On the friezes of the Parthenon and the remains of the earliest Greek art.

On marriage

Is not marriage an open question when it is alleged from the beginning of the world that such as are in the institution wish to get out and such as are out wish to get in?

The betrothed and accepted lover has lost the wildest charms of his maiden by her acceptance. She was heaven while he pursued her but she cannot be heaven if she stoops to One such as he!

On art

72

The martyr cannot be dishonored. Every lash inflicted is a tongue of fame; every prison a more illustrious abode.

The torments of martyrdom are probably most keenly felt by the bystanders.

On masses

The masses have no habit of self- reliance or original action.

Leave this hypocritical prating about the masses. Masses are rude lame unmade pernicious in their demands and influence and need not to be flattered but to be schooled. I wish not to concede anything to them but to tame drill divide and break them up and draw individuals out of them.

On men

Men are what their mothers made them.

Men cease to interest us when we find their limitations.

On women

Let us treat the men and women well: treat them as if they were real: perhaps they are.

On mentors

My chief want in life is someone who shall make me do what I can.

We boast our emancipation from many superstitions; but if we have broken any idols it is through a transfer of idolatry.

On mind

He then learns that in going down into the secrets of his own mind he has descended into the secrets of all minds.

We cannot see things that stare us in the face until the hour comes that the mind is ripened.

On minorities

Shall we judge a country by the majority or by the minority? By the minority surely.

All history is a record of the power of minorities and of minorities of One.

On mobs

The mob is man voluntarily descending to the nature of the beast. Its fit hour of activity is night. Its actions are insane like its whole constitution. It persecutes a principle; it would whip a right; it would tar and feather justice by inflicting fire and outrage upon the houses and persons of those who have these. It resembles the prank of boys who run with fire-engines to put out the ruddy aurora streaming to the stars.

On money

The world is his who has money to go over it.

Money often costs too much.

Money is the representative of a certain quantity of corn or other commodity. It is so much warmth so much bread.

It requires a great deal of boldness and a great deal of caution to make a great fortune and when you have it requires ten times as much skill to keep it.

Money which represents the prose of life and which is hardly spoken of in parlors without an apology is in its effects and laws as beautiful as roses.

On morality

The fatal trait of the times is the divorce between religion and morality.

On motivation

If you would lift me up you must be on higher ground.

On murder

Murder in the murderer is no such ruinous thought as poets and romancers will have it; it does not unsettle him or fright him from his ordinary notice of trifles; it is an act quite easy to be contemplated.

On music

Music causes us to think eloquently.

N

On nature

Nature is an endless combination and repetition of a very few laws. She hums the old well-known air through innumerable variations.

A man is related to all nature.

Nature is a mutable cloud which is always and never the same.

Nature has made up her mind that what cannot defend itself shall not be defended.

Everything in Nature contains all the powers of Nature. Everything is made of hidden stuff.

In nature nothing can be given. All things are sold.

The rich mind lies in the sun and sleeps and is Nature.

On nature

We fly to beauty as an asylum from the terrors of finite nature.

To the dull mind all nature is leaden. To the illumined mind the whole world burns and sparkles with light.

Nature... She pardons no mistakes. Her yea is yea and her nay nay

On necessity

Make yourself necessary to somebody.

By necessity by proclivity and by delight we all . In fact it is as difficult to appropriate the thoughts of others as it is to invent.

Necessity does everything well.

We do what we must and call it by the best names.

On nicknames

No orator can top the one who can give good nicknames.

O

On obedience

The reason why men do not obey us is because they see the mud at the bottom of our eye.

On obstacles

As long as a man stands in his own way everything seems to be in his way.

On opinions

Stay at home in your mind. Don't recite other people's opinions. I hate quotations. Tell me what you know.

The Only sin that we never forgive in each other is a difference in opinion.

On opportunity

Be an opener of doors.

Never lose an opportunity of seeing anything that is beautiful; for beauty is God's handwriting -- a wayside sacrament. Welcome it in every fair face in every fair sky in every fair flower and thank God for it as a cup of blessing.

If a man can write a better book preach a better sermon or make a better mousetrap than his neighbor though he build his house in the woods the world will make a beaten path to his door.

Every wall is a door.

On opposites

Every sweet has its sour; every evil its good.

P

On parents and parenting

Is the parent better than the child into whom he has cast his ripened being?
Whence then this worship of the past?

On power

The education of the will is the object of our existence.

On passion

Passion though a bad regulator is a powerful spring.

On patience

Adopt the pace of nature; her secret is patience.

On peace

Peace cannot be achieved through violence it can only be attained through understanding.

Peace has its victories but it takes brave men and women to win them.

Nothing can bring you peace but yourself; nothing but the triumph of principles.

On people

The people are to be taken in small doses.

Other men are lenses through which we read our own minds. Each man seeks those of different quality from his own and such as are good of their kind; that is he seeks other men and the rest.

It is hard to go beyond your public. If they are satisfied with cheap performance you will not easily arrive at better. If they know what is good and require it. you will aspire and burn until you achieve it. But from time to time in history men are born a whole age too soon.

On performance

The history of persecution is a history of endeavors to cheat nature to make water run up hill to twist a rope of sand.

On perseverance

By persisting in your path though you forfeit the little you gain the great.

On persuasion

That which we do not believe we cannot adequately say; even though we may repeat the words ever so often.

On philanthropists

The worst of charity is that the lives you are asked to preserve are not worth preserving.

On philosophers and philosophy

Out of Plato come all things that are still written and debated about among men of thought.

On plagiarism

Genius Borrows nobly.

On planning

To map out a course of action and follow it to an end requires some of the same courage that a soldier needs.

Few people have any next they live from hand to mouth without a plan and are always at the end of their line.

On pleasure

Whenever you are sincerely pleased you are nourished.

On poetry and poets

It does not need that a poem should be long. Every word was Once a poem. Every new relationship is a new word.

Only poetry inspires poetry.

Painting was called silent poetry and poetry speaking painting.

Poetry must be as new as foam and as old as the rock.

Sooner or later that which is now life shall be poetry and every fair and manly trait shall add a richer strain to the song.

On politics

There is a certain satisfaction in coming down to the lowest ground of politics for we get rid of cant and hypocrisy.

On population

If government knew how I should like to see it check not multiply the population. When it reaches its true law of action every man that is born will be hailed as essential.

On possessions

Some men are born to own and can animate all their possessions. Others cannot: their owning is not graceful; seems to be a compromise of their character: they seem to steal their own dividends.

On possibilities

We have more than we use.

The power which resides in man is new in nature and none but he knows what that is which he can do nor does he know until he has tried.

Every man believes that he has greater possibilities.

Oh man! There is no planet sun or star could hold you if you but knew what you are.

On poverty and the poor

Poverty consists in feeling poor.

The greatest man in history was the poorest.

The creation of a thousand forest in one acorn.

On power

Nature arms each man with some faculty which enables him to do easily some feat impossible to any other.

The stupidity of men always invites the insolence of power.

A good indignation brings out all One's powers.

Do the thing and you will have the power. But they that do not the thing had not the power.

Wherever there is power there is age.

What lies behind you and what lies in front of you pales in comparison to what lies inside of you.

There is no knowledge that is not power.

On praise

When I was praised I lost my time for instantly I turned around to look at the work I had thought slightly of and that day I made nothing new.

Some natures are too good to be spoiled by praise.

On preachers and preaching

Preaching is the expression of moral sentiments applied to the duties of life.

The good rain like a bad preacher does not know when to leave off.

On present

Today is a king in disguise.

Those who live to the future must always appear selfish to those who live to the present.

Give me insight into today and you may have the antique and future worlds.

Finish each day before you begin the next and interpose a solid wall of sleep between the two. This you cannot do without temperance.

On presidents

The President has paid dear for his White House. It has commonly cost him all his peace and the best of his manly attributes. To preserve for a short time so conspicuous an appearance before the world he is content to eat dust before the real masters who stand erect behind the throne.

On progress

The walking of Man is falling forwards.

On progress

All our progress is an unfolding like a vegetable bud. You have first an instinct then an opinion then a knowledge as the plant has root bud and fruit. Trust the instinct to the end though you can render no reason.

On promises

All promise outruns performance.

On property

No man acquires property without acquiring with it a little arithmetic also.

If a man owns land the land owns him.

Property is an intellectual production. The game requires coolness right reasoning promptness and patience in the players.

On purpose

I know of no such unquestionable badge and ensign of a sovereign mind as that of tenacity of purpose...

Men achieve a certain greatness unawares when working to another aim.

On pursuit

The crowning fortune of a man is to be born to some pursuit which finds him employment and happiness whether it be to make baskets or broadswords or canals or statues or songs.

Q

On quality

The artists must be sacrificed to their art. Like the bees they must put their lives into the sting they give.

On quotations

The next best thing to saying a good thing yourself is to one.

The profoundest thought or passion sleeps as in a mine until an equal mind and heart finds and publishes it.

I hate quotations. Tell me what you know.

Next to the originator of a good sentence is the first r of it. Many will read the book before One thinks of quoting a passage. As soon as he has done this that line will be d east and west.

The adventitious beauty of poetry may be felt in the greater delight with a verse given in a happy quotation than in the poem.

He presents me with what is always an acceptable gift who brings me news of a great thought before unknown. He enriches me without impoverishing himself.

Some men's words I remember so well that I must often use them to express my thought. Yes because I perceive that we have heard the same truth but they have heard it better.

R

On radicals

The spirit of our American radicalism is destructive and aimless; it is not loving; it has no ulterior and divine ends; but is destructive Only out of hatred and selfishness.

On reality

You cannot do wrong without suffering wrong.

On reform

Every reform was Once a private opinion and when it shall be a private opinion again it will solve the problem of the age.

On rejection

Dear to us are those who love us... but dearer are those who reject us as unworthy for they add another life; they build a heaven before us whereof we had not dreamed and thereby supply to us new powers out of the recesses of the spirit and urge us to new and unattempted performances.

On religion

The religion that is afraid of science dishonors God and commits suicide.

On respectability

Men are respectable only as they respect.

On riches

Man was born to be rich or grow rich by use of his faculties by the union of thought with nature. Property is an intellectual production. The game requires coolness right reasoning promptness and patience in the players.

On risk

I dip my pen in the blackest ink because I am not afraid of falling into my inkpot.

On rumors

We must set up a strong present tense against all rumors of wrath past and to come.

On recognition

The silence that accepts merit as the most natural thing in the world is the highest applause.

S

On sympathy

Sympathy is a supporting atmosphere and in it we unfold easily and well.

On safety

In skating over thin ice our safety is in our speed.

On scholars and scholarship

I cannot forgive a scholar his homeless despondency.

The office of the scholar is to cheer to raise and to guide men by showing them facts amidst appearances. He plies the slow unhonored and unpaid task of observation. He is the world's eye.

On science

What terrible questions we are learning to ask! The former men believed in magic by which temples cities and men were swallowed up and all trace of them gone. We are coming On the secret of a magic which sweeps out of men's minds all vestige of theism and beliefs which they and their fathers held and were framed upon.

Do what we can summer will have its flies.

On sea

The sea washing the equator and the poles offers its perilous aid and the power and empire that follow it... Beware of me it says but if you can hold me I am the key to all the lands.

On security

No One has a prosperity so high and firm that two or three words can't dishearten it.

Nothing is secure but life transition the energizing spirit.

On self-esteem

Whatever games are played with us we must play no games with ourselves.

It is very easy in the world to live by the opinion of the world. It is very easy in solitude to be self-centered. But the finished man is he who in the midst of the crowd keeps with perfect sweetness the independence of solitude.

It is easy to live for others everybody does. I call on you to live for yourselves.

On self-expression

Insist On yourself; never imitate. Your own gift you can present every moment with the cumulative force of a whole life's cultivation; but of the adopted talent of another you haveoOnly an extemporaneous half possession.

On self-improvement

The never-ending task of self-improvement.

Welcome evermore to gods and men is the self-helping man. For him all doors are flung wide: him all tongues greet all honors crown all eyes follow with desire. Our love goes out to him and embraces him because he did not need it. We solicitously and apologetically caress and celebrate him because he held On his way and scorned our disapprobation. The gods loved him because men hated him.

On self-reliance

This gives force to the strong -- that the multitude have no habit of self-reliance or original action.

The best lightning rod for your protection is your own spine.

No One can cheat you out of ultimate success but yourself.

Self-reliance is its aversion. It loves not realities and creators but names and customs.

On self-respect

Let a man then know his worth and keep things under his feet. Let him not peep or steal or skulk up and down with the air of a charity-boy a bastard or an interloper.

On sacrifice

Self-sacrifice is the real miracle out of which all the reported miracles grow.

On self-trust

Self-trust is the first secret to success.

On time

Society is infested by persons who seeing that the sentiments please counterfeit the expression of them. These we call sentimentalists--talkers who mistake the description for the thing saying for having.

On service

He is great who confers the most benefits.

No man can help another without helping himself.

On silence

Let us be silent that we may hear the whispers of the gods.

On simplicity

Nothing is more simple than greatness; indeed to be simple is to be great.

It the proof of high culture to say the greatest matters in the simplest way.

On sin

That which we call sin in others is experiment for us.

On sincerity

Every man alone is sincere. At the entrance of a second person hypocrisy begins.

Sincerity is the luxury allowed like diadems and authority Only to the highest rank. Every man alone is sincere. At the entrance of a second person hypocrisy begins.

Sincerity is the highest compliment you can pay

On skepticism

Skepticism is unbelief in cause and effect.

On sky

The sky is the daily bread of the eyes.

On slavery

Slavery is an institution for converting men into monkeys.

On society

Society never advances. It recedes as fast on one side as it gains on the other. Society acquires new arts and loses old instincts.

Society is a hospital of incurables.

Society always consists in the greatest part of young and foolish persons.

Society everywhere is in conspiracy against the manhood of every one of its members. The virtue in most request is conformity. Self-reliance is its aversion. It loves not realities and creators but names and customs.

Society is a masked ball where everyone hides his real character and reveals it by hiding.

On solitude

It is easy in the world to live after the world's opinions; it is easy in solitude to live after your own; but the great man is he who in the midst of the crowd keeps with perfect sweetness the independence of solitude.

Solitude is impractical and yet society is fatal.

We walk alone in the world.

We never touch but at points.

Conversation enriches the understanding; but solitude is the school of genius.

On sorrow

Sorrow makes us children again.

The Only thing grief as taught me is to know how shallow it is.

Sorrow makes us all children again destroys all differences of intellect. The wisest knows nothing.

On soul

The one thing in the world of value is the active soul.

The soul's emphasis is always right.

On speakers and speaking

All the great speakers were bad speakers at first.

Condense some daily experience into a glowing symbol and an audience is electrified.

On speech

Speech is power: speech is to persuade to convert to compel. It is to bring another out of his bad sense into your good sense.

On spirituality

The foundations of a person are not in matter but in spirit.

On spontaneity

Our spontaneous action is always the best. You cannot with your best deliberation and heed come so close to any question as your spontaneous glance shall bring you.

On state

The State must follow and not lead the character and progress of the citizen.

On strength

We acquire the strength we have overcome.

There is always room for a person of force and they make room for many.

On stupidity

The key to the age may be this or that or the other as the young orators describe; the key to all ages is -- Imbecility; imbecility in the vast majority of men at all times and even in heroes in all but certain eminent moments; victims of gravity custom and fear.

On success

To laugh often and much; to win the respect of intelligent people and the affection of children; to earn the appreciation of honest critics and endure the betrayal of false friends; to appreciate beauty; to find the best in others; to leave the world a bit better whether by a healthy child a garden patch or a redeemed social condition; to know even One life has breathed easier because you have lived. This is to have succeeded.

Often a certain abdication of prudence and foresight is an element of success.

A strenuous soul hates cheap success.

If man has good corn or wood or boards or pigs to sell or can make better chairs or knives crucibles or church organs than anybody else you will find a broad hard-beaten road to his house though it be in the woods.

There is no way to success in art but to take off your coat grind paint and work like a digger On the railroad all day and every day.

On snow

Announced by all the trumpets of the sky arrives the snow.

On sailing

The wonder is always new that any sane man can be a sailor.

The most advanced nations are always those who navigate the most.

T

On talent

Every man has his own vocation talent is the call.

It is a happy talent to know how to play.

Talent alone cannot make a writer. There must be a man behind the book; a personality which by birth and quality is pledged to the doctrines there set forth and which exists to see and state things so and not otherwise.

Talent for talent's sake is a bauble and a show. Talent working with joy in the cause of universal truth lifts the possessor to new power as a benefactor.

Talent is commonly developed at the expense of character.

On talkativeness

What you do speaks so loud that I cannot hear what you say.

On taste

A man is known by the books he reads by the company he keeps by the praise he gives by his dress by his tastes by his distastes by the stories he tells by his gait by the notion of his eye by the look of his house of his chamber; for nothing On earth is solitary but everything hath affinities infinite.

On taxes and taxation

Every advantage has its tax.

The man who can make hard things easy is the educator.

On teachers

Knowledge exists to be imparted.

On temper

Men lose their tempers in defending their taste.

On temptation

We gain the strength of the temptation we resist.

On thoughts and thinking

What your heart thinks is great is great. The soul's emphasis is always right.

If a man sits down to think he is immediately asked if has a headache.

Life consists in what a person is thinking of all day.

Some thoughts always find us young and keep us so. Such a thought is the love of the universal and eternal beauty.

The key to every man is his thought. Sturdy and defying though he look he has a helm which he obeys which is the idea after which all his facts are classified. He can Only be reformed by showing him a new idea which commands his own.

The revelation of Thought takes men out of servitude into freedom.

The soul of God is poured into the world through the thoughts of men.

There is no thought in any mind but it quickly tends to convert itself into power.

Thought makes everything fit for use.

To think is to act.

A sect or party is an incognito devised to save man from the vexation of thinking.

A man's what he thinks about all day long

We are ashamed of our thoughts and often see them brought forth by others.

Beware when the great God lets loose a thinker On this planet.

What is the hardest thing in the world? To think.

On time

One of the illusions of life is that the present hour is not the critical decisive hour. Write it on your heart that every day is the best day in the year. No man has learned anything rightly until he knows that every day is Doomsday.

This time like all times is a very good One if we but know what to do with it.

These times of ours are serious and full of calamity but all times are essentially alike. As soon as there is life there is danger.

The surest poison is time.

So much of our time is spent in preparation so much in routine and so much in retrospect that the amount of each person's genius is confined to a very few hours.

On trade

The greatest meliorator of the world is selfish huckstering Trade.

We rail at trade but the historian of the world will see that it was the principle of liberty; that it settled America and destroyed feudalism and made peace and keeps peace; that it will abolish slavery.

On translation

I do not hesitate to read all good books in translations. What is really best in any book is translatable -- any real insight or broad human sentiment.

On Travel

I am not much an advocate for traveling and I observe that men run away to other countries because they are not good in their own and run back to their own because they pass for nothing in the new places. For the most part Only the light characters travel. Who are you that have no task to keep you at home?

Traveling is a fool's paradise. Our first journeys discover to us the indifference of places.

Travel is a fool's paradise.

Though we travel the world over to find the beautiful we must carry it with us or we find it not.

No man should travel until he has learned the language of the country he visits. Otherwise he voluntarily makes himself a great baby-so helpless and so ridiculous.

On trust

Trust men and they will be true to you; treat them greatly and they will show themselves great.

Trust thyself: every heart vibrates to that iron string.

Trust instinct to the end even though you can give no reason.

The highest compact we can make with our fellow is --Let there be truth between us two forevermore.

Self-trust is the essence of heroism.

All I have seen teaches me to trust the creator for all I have not seen.

On truth

Truth is the property of no individual but is the treasure of all men.

Truth is the summit of being; justice is the application of it to affairs.

Truth is beautiful without doubt; but so are lies.

The greatest homage we can pay truth is to use it.

Every mind has a choice between truth and repose. Take which you please you can never have both.

All necessary truth is its own evidence.

7

U

On ugliness

The secret of ugliness consists not in irregularity but in being uninteresting.

On understanding

No man thoroughly understands a truth until he has contended against it.

On uniqueness

Is the acorn better than the oak which is its fullness and completion?

On upbringing

I suffer whenever I see that common sight of a parent or senior imposing his opinion and way of thinking and being on a young soul to which they are totally unfit. Cannot we let people be themselves and enjoy life in their own way? You are trying to make that man another you. One's enough.

V

On valor

There is always safety in valor.

Valor consists in the power of self- recovery.

On value

The value of a principle is the number of things it will explain; and there is no good theory of disease which does not at Once suggest a cure.

On victory

Wherever work is done victory is attained.

The god of victory is said to be One-handed but peace gives victory On both sides.

No matter how often you are defeated you are born to victory.

Men talk as if victory were something fortunate. Work is victory.

On villains

As there is a use in medicine for poisons so the world cannot move without rogues.

On virtue

The virtues of society are vices of the saint. The terror of reform is the discovery that we must cast away our virtues or what we have always esteemed such into the same pit that has consumed our grosser vices.

A weed is a plant whose virtues have not yet been discovered.

What is a weed? A plant whose virtues have not yet been discovered

The virtue in most request is conformity.

The Only reward of virtue is virtue.

The less a man thinks or knows about his virtues the better we like him.

Hitch your wagon to a star. Let us not lag in paltry works which serve our pot and bag alone.

Commerce is of trivial import; love faith truth of character the aspiration of man these are sacred.

Do not follow where the path may lead. Go instead where there is no path and leave a trail.

A man's style is his mind's voice. Wooden minds wooden voices.

Words so vascular and alive they would bleed if you cut them words that walked and ran.

On War

The triumphs of peace have been in some proximity to war. Whilst the hand was still familiar with the sword-hilt whilst the habits of the camp were still visible in the port and complexion of the gentleman his intellectual power culminated; the compression and tension of these stern conditions is a training for the finest and softest arts and can rarely be compensated in tranquil times except by some analogous vigor drawn from occupations as hardy as war.

It is One of the most beautiful compensations in life that no man can sincerely try to help another without helping himself.

On want

Want is a growing giant whom the coat of Have was never large enough to cover.

On weakness

Our strength grows out of our weakness.

On well

The reward of a thing well done is to have done it.

On wealth

The first wealth is health.

Without a rich heart wealth is an ugly beggar.

On wisdom

Wealth is in applications of mind to nature; and the art of getting rich consists not in industry much less in saving but in a better order in timeliness in being at the right spot.

Raphael paints wisdom; Handel sings it Phidias carves it Shakespeare writes it Wren builds it Columbus sails it Luther preaches it Washington arms it Watt mechanizes it.

Wisdom is like electricity. There is no permanently wise man but men capable of wisdom who being put into certain company or other favorable conditions become wise for a short time as glasses rubbed acquire electric power for a while.

Let us be poised and wise and our own today.

Life is a festival only to the wise.

There is a time when a man distinguishes the idea of felicity from the idea of wealth; it is the beginning of wisdom.

On wish and wishing

There is no beautifier of complexion or form of behavior like the wish to scatter joy and not pain around us.

Beware what you set your heart upon. For it shall surely be yours.

On wit

Wit makes its own welcome and levels all distinctions. No dignity no learning no force of character can make any stand against good wit.

On wives

A man's wife has more power over him than the state has.

On women

Slavery it is that makes slavery; freedom. The slavery of women happened when the men were slaves of kings.

On wonder

Men love to wonder and that is the seed of our science.

On words

It makes a great difference in the force of a sentence whether a man be behind it or no.

Words are alive; cut them and they bleed.

On work

See only that thou work and thou canst not escape the reward.

We must hold a man amenable to reason for the choice of his daily craft or profession. It is not an excuse any longer for his deeds that they are the custom of his trade. What business has he with an evil trade?

Work and thou canst escape the reward; whether the work be fine or course planting corn or writing epics so Only it be honest work done to thine own approbation it shall earn a reward to the senses as well as to the thought.
  On work

Work is victory.

On the world

The mark of the man of the world is absence of pretension. He does not make a speech; he takes a low business-tone avoids all brag is nobody dresses plainly promises not at all performs much speaks in monosyllables hugs his fact. He calls his employment by its lowest name and so takes from evil tongues their sharpest weapon. His conversation clings to the weather and the news yet he allows himself to be surprised into thought and the unlocking of his learning and philosophy.

On worry

Little minds have little worries big minds have no time for worries.

On writers and writing

There is no luck in literary reputation. They who make up the final verdict upon every book are not the partial and noisy readers of the hour when it appears; but a court as of angels a public not to be bribed not to be entreated and not to be overawed decides upon every man's title to fame.

Emerson's study

14149130R00065

Made in the USA
Lexington, KY
15 March 2012